It's another Quality Book from CGP

This Teacher Book is perfect for helping you get the most out of CGP's Year 5 Word Power Book.

It contains a huge range of useful teaching resources, including example answers to each question, extra background material, suggestions for scaffolding and extension activities... plus much more.

What CGP is all about

Our sole aim here at CGP is to produce the highest quality books — carefully written, immaculately presented and dangerously close to being funny.

Then we work our socks off to get them out to you — at the cheapest possible prices.

Language Families

2

Section 1 — Words At War

Language Families

Did you know that languages belong in families? Most of the languages spoken in Europe belong to an extended family called 'Indo-European'. They have developed from an original language spoken over 5,000 years ago.

As the Indo-European people moved around Europe thousands of years ago, their language changed and developed into lots of different languages. Look at this simplified family tree, which shows how languages kept branching off. It shows the word 'night' in the different languages.

- **Indo-European** — nokwts
  - **Latin** — nox
    - **French** — nuit
    - **Italian** — notte
  - **Low German** — nahts
    - **German** — Nacht
    - **English** — night

Latin is a mother language of French and Italian. What can you say about the relationship between English and German?

Look at the table below. Can you guess what the English words are?

Indo-European word	French word	German word	English word
nas	nez	Nase	n o s e
pisk	poisson	Fisch	f i s h
wodr	eau	Wasser	w a t e r
brehter	frère	Bruder	b r o t h e r

Do you notice any similarities in the way these words are spelt?

Are the English words in the table above more similar to the French or German words? Why might this be?

Think about the family relationships between the languages.

The English words are more similar to the German words. I think this is because English and German share the same parent language — Low German.

Extra Background

Certain words from Indo-European, like 'mother', 'night', 'moon', and 'wolf', have survived relatively unchanged in most modern European languages.

Pupil Guidance

English and German are sibling languages. They share the same parent language — Low German.

Pupil Guidance

Words that have changed relatively little are usually those that are important to human survival or family relationships.

Suggested Scaffolding

Encourage students to say the German words aloud if they are struggling to guess what the English words are.

Extension Idea

Pupils can use the concept of early human beings developing words for the things that are important to them to create a story or poem about what it might have been like to be a Stone, Bronze or Iron Age person.

Language Families — Aims:

- to enable pupils to understand that some languages spoken today developed from Indo-European
- to give pupils an understanding of Germanic and Romance language families.

3

The family tree shows us that English belongs to the <u>Germanic</u> family of languages. Languages which come from Latin are called <u>Romance</u> languages. The map below shows where these two different families of languages are spoken.

Can you put each language into the correct language family?

🇩🇰 Danish   Dutch   🇬🇧 English   🇫🇷 French   German   🇮🇹 Italian

🇳🇴 Norwegian   Romanian   Portuguese   Spanish   🇸🇪 Swedish

North

■ Germanic
■ Romance

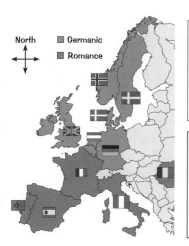

Germanic Languages
English Dutch German Swedish Danish Norwegian.

Romance Languages
Italian French Romanian Spanish Portuguese.

Look at the map above. What do you notice about the location of Germanic languages and Romance languages?

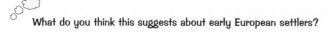
I notice that most of the Germanic languages are in the north and west of Europe, and that most of the Romance languages are in the south of Europe.

What do you think this suggests about early European settlers?

What have you learnt about language families?

I understand that English is a Germanic language, and some of our words are like German words.

Section 1 — Words At War

Extra Background

An example of another language family can be found in the Celtic languages. This family includes: Welsh, Irish, Scottish Gaelic and Breton (which is spoken in Brittany, Northern France).

Extension Idea

Ask children to use a translation program on the Internet to look at common words in other languages, and see if they look similar to the equivalent English word.

Pupil Guidance

Pupils should understand that when people move, languages move too. As early European settlers moved about the continent and settled in different locations, their original languages began to change until they developed into separate languages.

Pupil Guidance

Ask pupils to think about language relationships, looking back at the family tree on page 2.

Word Invasions

4

Word Invasions

Britain has been invaded several times over the centuries, and each group of invaders has influenced the language we speak today. The Romans invaded in 43, then almost 400 years later, the Saxons invaded and settled in Britain. After the Saxons, the Vikings invaded in about 800, and in 1066 the Normans invaded!

The Romans spoke Latin, and some Latin words have survived in English from when the Romans invaded. Can you work out what the English versions of these Latin words are?

portus → p o r t

strata → s t r e e t

castellum → c a s t l e

Are these words connected? Do these words tell you anything about the Romans?

The Saxons and the Vikings spoke Germanic languages. Here are some words from the Saxons and the Vikings that we still use today.

and, like, before, bring, can, see, do, find, go, have, I, to

take, sky, angry, both, call, dirt, egg, flat, get, happy, ill

How would you describe these words which have survived into modern English? Think about how they sound, and also what they are used for.

Think about how often you use these words.

 These words are quite short. They are words that we use every day.

In 1066, William of Normandy conquered England. William and his army spoke a Romance language called <u>Norman French</u>.

What do you think might happen to the languages when one set of people conquer another? Think about both the language of the conquer<u>ors</u>, and the language of the conquer<u>ed</u>.

 The language of the conquered people might die out or change because the conquerors force people to use their own language.

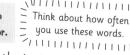

Word Invasions — Aims:

- to give pupils an understanding of how language in England developed as a result of invasions from the Romans to the Normans
- to show pupils how Latin words came into English through Norman French
- to enable pupils to understand why English is still considered a Germanic language.

Norman French descended from Latin, so we can trace how words came from Latin into Norman French, and then into English. Look at the words below. Can you work out what the modern English words are?

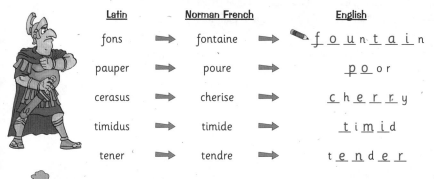

Latin	Norman French	English
fons	fontaine	f o u n t a i n
pauper	poure	p o o r
cerasus	cherise	c h e r r y
timidus	timide	t i m i d
tener	tendre	t e n d e r

These words have travelled a long way — from Rome, to Normandy, then to England. Are you surprised by how **much** or by how **little** these words have changed along the way?

Pupil Guidance
Pupils may notice that 'pauper' is a word in modern English, meaning 'poor person'. This is an example of a 'doublet', where we have two words in English from the same root. See page 9 for more on doublets. Similarly, 'font' comes from the Latin word 'fons'.

Below is a timeline showing when words came to Britain. Fill in the boxes with a few examples from these pages of words which have come into English from the different languages.

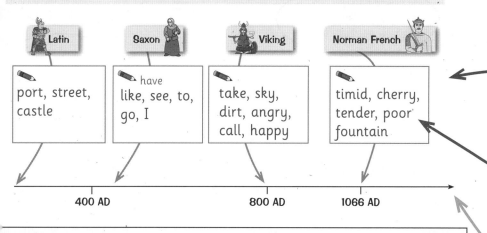

Latin: port, street, castle

Saxon: have, like, see, to, go, I

Viking: take, sky, dirt, angry, call, happy

Norman French: timid, cherry, tender, poor, fountain

400 AD   800 AD   1066 AD

Suggested Scaffolding
Encourage children to refer back to page 4.

Pupil Guidance
This is only a selection of the possible answers.

English contains lots of words that come from Latin roots. Why do you think it is still called a 'Germanic' language?

Because most of the words that are used everyday are from German roots, either through the Vikings or the Saxons.

Extension Idea
Pupils could extend this timeline by adding examples of words that have come into English during recent years.

Section 1 — Words At War

Pupil Guidance
Pupils might also say that English has descended from Low German which is a Germanic language.

William's Words

Extra Background

William of Normandy replaced Saxon landowners with his own men as a reward for their services in battle.

Suggested Scaffolding

Some students might understand this concept more clearly if they are given a different scenario. Imagine that aliens, who speak the language Zorg, have taken over Earth. How would humans react to the alien invaders and their language?

Extra Background

The Norman French word for pig was 'porc'. This was also their word for the meat of a pig. So they'd have said: "There's a 'porc' in the field" and "there's some 'porc' on the plate".

6

William's Words

William of Normandy and his army had a huge impact on the Saxons living in Britain. William's language had a huge impact too.

Look at the scene below between a Norman knight and a Saxon peasant.

"O paysan, auroi ce porc, mercy!"
"OK peasant, I'll have that pig, thanks!"

The knight is speaking Norman French and the Saxon is speaking Old English.

"Heo waes min swín! Agiefe me min swín!"
"That was my pig! Give me my pig!"

What does it suggest about the relationship between the Normans and the Saxons? Circle the sentences you think apply.

It was hard for the Saxons and Normans to understand each other.

The Saxons and the Normans understood each other's language.

The Normans were more powerful.

The Saxons were more powerful.

The Saxons would need to learn Norman words.

Think about the sentences you have circled above. How would you feel if you were a Saxon and had to speak the language of the people who had conquered you?

I might feel angry

because I wouldn't be able to speak my language if I wanted to talk to the people who were in charge.

Within a few years, the Normans had changed England completely. If you were a Saxon, you didn't have much power or much land. If you wanted to be an important person, you had to speak Norman French.

© CGP — not to be photocopie

Extension Idea

Ask pupils what they call a 'cow' or a 'sheep' when it's on the plate ('beef' and 'mutton'). Tell pupils that 'beef' and 'mutton' entered the language from Norman French and that 'cow' and 'sheep' come from Saxon words. What does this suggest about who ate the meat and who looked after the animals?

William's Words — Aims:

- to demonstrate to pupils how the Saxon and Norman languages interacted after the Norman conquest
- to give pupils an understanding of the social implications of the Norman conquest through language.

7

The Normans were here to stay, so they needed to find a way to communicate with the Saxons. How do you think the language spoken by the Saxons changed after the Norman invasion?

✎ After the Norman invasion, the Saxons might have started to use more Norman French words.

Sort the modern English words below into two groups — words ordinary people would use every day, and words that would be used to rule a country.

If you don't know what a word means, use a dictionary to look it up!

moral sky traitor

cry dream house

meat ~~milk~~ punishment

apple anger ~~convict~~

discussion court

bread buy run hope

Everyday Words

✎ milk

sky   cry

dream   house

meat   bread

buy   run

hope   apple

anger

Ruling a Country Words

✎ convict

moral   traitor

punishment

discussion

court

One set of words comes from the Saxons, and the other set comes from the Normans. No prizes for guessing which was which!

How did the English language change once its people had been conquered by the Normans?

✎ It added many words that were used by the Normans to govern the people, but kept Saxon words for daily life.

Section 1 — Words At War

Extra Background

Eventually the two languages — Norman French and Old English — combined to form Middle English.

Pupil Guidance

All of the everyday words (except 'anger' and 'apple') are monosyllabic. Most of the Norman words in the right-hand box are polysyllabic.

Pupil Guidance

The 'everyday' words come from Saxon and the 'ruling' words come from Norman French.

Extra Background

The Normans began to use Saxon words as the Normans and Saxons married, and children grew up knowing both languages. Children are important in the process of integrating one language with another. They pick up new words and ideas more quickly than older people.

Latin Survives

8

Latin Survives

Latin didn't have any native speakers by the 900s — no one spoke it as their first language. But it continued to play an important role in European life. Let's see how!

In the year 842, two kings promised to support each other. One king was from what is now Germany, the other was from what is now France.

In front of their armies, they made their promises to each other in each other's language. Their armies made a promise in their own languages.

However, the document recording the event was mainly written in Latin.

What does this suggest about Latin at this time? Have a think about each of the statements below. Tick whether you Agree, Disagree or Can't Tell.

	Agree	Disagree	Can't Tell
"Latin was used for important documents."	✔	☐	☐
"Neither king could understand Latin."	☐	☐	✔
"Latin was used for writing."	✔	☐	☐
"Latin was an international language."	✔	☐	☐
"Everyone could speak two languages."	☐	☐	✔
"Latin was used as a neutral language."	✔	☐	☐

'Neutral' here means not belonging to either side.

For centuries, Latin was used throughout Europe as the language of the Church. If you were a Saxon who couldn't understand Latin, how would you feel about having to listen to Latin in church?

I think I would ✎ wonder why I couldn't listen to a service in a language that I understood.

Latin was given a big boost in the 1400s when scholars rediscovered lots of Latin books from Roman times, which hadn't been read for hundreds of years. Suddenly it was new and exciting to speak, write and read Latin.

This period is called the <u>Renaissance</u>, which means 'rebirth'.

Extra Background

The Oaths of Strasbourg in 842 were pledges of mutual defence between two half-brothers holding different territories. The oaths they took were in their own languages — Old French, and Old German, because it was considered that everyone should understand what they were promising.

Extension Idea

Pupils might give different answers. Discuss any alternative answers as a class.

Suggested Scaffolding

A different scenario might be helpful if pupils struggle to think of an answer. Imagine that your teachers have decided to teach all their lessons in Latin. How would that make you feel? Do you think you'd still be able to learn as much as you do now?

Extension Idea

Research Elizabeth I to investigate how important speaking different languages was in the Renaissance. She spoke and read six!

Latin Survives — Aims:

- to allow pupils to investigate how Latin remained an important language across Europe, especially for the Church and as a written language
- to demonstrate to pupils the ways in which Latin words continued to flow into English, creating 'doublets'.

9

So Latin really came into fashion during the Renaissance. How do you think lots more people reading Latin would have affected the English language?

After the Renaissance, more words came into English from Latin roots. In many cases, English already had words from these Latin roots, so English ended up with two words from the same root.

These are called 'doublets'.

Latin word

dignitas

dainty   dignity

Below are some more doublets. Can you think of the missing word in each doublet? Look up all the words in a dictionary and write their definitions on the lines.

fragilis
→ frail — Weak
→ fra g i l e — Easily breakable

potio
→ poison — Something bad for you
→ p o t i o n — A liquid that can heal, or is magical

securus
→ sure — When you know something will happen
→ s e c u re — Safely put away, or kept

These pairs of words mean different things but their meanings are related.
Pick one pair of words, and explain in your own words how their meanings are similar.

Frail and fragile are both to do with something not very strong. Poison and potion are both something you might drink. Sure and secure are both to do with being safe.

How did Latin survive in Britain despite having no native speakers?

Latin survived because of the Church, and because it was used by educated people.

Extra Background

The Renaissance was a time of renewed interest in learning, and many texts in Latin and Greek came into Britain through universities.

Suggested Scaffolding

Encourage pupils to try writing these words out in different sentences — this may help them to distinguish the difference in meaning.

Pupil Guidance

Pupils will give slightly different definitions for these words, which could act as another discussion point on shades of meaning.

Extension Idea

Encourage pupils to link the work on doublets with work on synonyms. They could use a thesaurus to investigate the shades of meaning in words that are similar.

Words On The Page

10

Extra Background

In 1841, 33% of men signing a marriage register in England, and 44% of women, had to make their mark (draw an 'x') instead of write their name, as they couldn't write. Prior to that, even fewer people could read or write. The adult literacy rate now in Britain is about 99%.

Pupil Guidance

The oral tradition of telling stories and singing ballads lived on while literacy developed alongside it. Eventually the stories were written down.

Extra Background

Illuminated manuscripts were often handwritten on vellum — a type of parchment made from animal hides. The process of making vellum was time-consuming and expensive. Most printed books were printed on paper.

Extension Idea

Investigate the lives of Johannes Gutenberg and William Caxton and how their work helped to develop book printing in Europe.

Words On The Page

Language isn't just spoken, it can be written down too. But it wasn't always written down. Let's take a look at how words came to be on the page...

Early English poetry was recited or sung, and wasn't written down until about 650. Why might people tell poems or stories rather than write them down?

I think they did this because ✎ _most people couldn't read or write._

Over 1,500 years ago most books were handwritten in Latin. They were written by monks who were living and working within the Church. We call their handwritten documents <u>manuscripts</u>.

There were problems with writing things down by hand. What do you think these problems could be? Tick all that apply — there's even space to write your own if you can think of any!

✎

| ✔ People could make mistakes. | ☐ It was boring. |
| ✔ It took a long time. | ✔ It was expensive. |

✎ _Making paper and ink might have been difficult._

Not everybody could read and write. Here are some occupations from the 1500s. Circle the ones who probably <u>would</u> have been able to read and write.

✎ (lawyer)   (scribe)   grocer

farmer   (nobleman)   peasant

Why do you think some people didn't need to be able to read or write?

Things began to change when William Caxton introduced the first printing press to England in 1476. William printed books of poetry, stories and works of philosophy — and most of them were printed in English, rather than Latin!

Pupil Guidance

People may not have needed to read or write because they could do everything they needed without it.

Words On The Page — Aims:

- to enable pupils to consider how books developed and who might have owned and used them
- to enable pupils to understand how the invention of printing affected literature and spelling
- to allow pupils to consider how the meanings of words in dictionaries can change over time.

11

Think about the things you use and see everyday that have been printed. Make a list of them here.

> posters   newspapers   books   leaflets   bus timetables
> magazines   cereal packets   milk cartons

How do you think the invention of the printing press changed the lives of ordinary people?

I think that the printing press probably didn't affect the lives of illiterate people too much. If you were literate, the printing press meant there were more books available in English.

Before the invention of the printing press, people used to spell words differently all the time. Why do you think the development of the printing press would improve people's spelling?

I think that before the printing press, different writers might spell the same word differently. After the printing press, writers might spell words the same as in printed books, so there would be less variation.

Dictionaries were also printed to help people with their spelling. But sometimes even the dictionary needs updating...

In 1755, a man called Dr Samuel Johnson published 'A Dictionary of the English Language'. This is his primary definition for the word 'keen'.

> **keen** *adj* [cene, Saxon]
> Sharp; well edged; not blunt.

Do you think this is the most widely used meaning of the word 'keen' nowadays? If not, what do you think the word 'keen' means?

No, I think nowadays the word 'keen' means you are interested in something.

From the 1500s onwards more books were being printed in English. What does this tell you about the importance of the English language?

I think that it means that English was becoming more important as a language, and French / Latin less important.

Pupil Guidance

Perhaps focus on certain areas in pupils' homes, such as the kitchen, and ask them to list everything they can think of.

Extra Background

Once the press was developed, printers began to standardise spellings. This was because they set individual letters made of lead into a wooden frame to compose words. It was easier to spell words the same way every time, rather than changing the letters.

Suggested Scaffolding

Pupils could look up the word 'keen' in the dictionary and discuss its different meanings.

Pupil Guidance

Words constantly change meanings and drop in and out of use. Pupils might like to ask older people for examples of words they seldom hear now.

Pupil Guidance

The split in the 1540s from the Roman Catholic Church, whose primary language was Latin, and wars with France also fuelled the rise of the English language.

Words From Latin

Extra Background

Latin is a 'dead language'. Although it is still used for certain documents and specific situations (e.g. the Church), no one speaks Latin as their native language.

Pupil Guidance

It's important to distinguish the meaning of similarly spelt prefixes. 'Anti', meaning 'against' or 'preventing', is not the same as 'ante', meaning 'before' or 'in front of'.

Pupil Guidance

Many of the prefixes will go with several different root words. Other answers could be 'retract', 'conspire', 'deflect', 'detract' or 'inscribe'.

Extension Idea

Ask pupils to create a set of prefix and suffix 'clouds' in their books. Get them to write as many words as they can using the prefixes and suffixes, but with different roots.

---

12   *Section 2 — Ancient Meanings*

Words From Latin

Sometimes you might come across a word that you don't recognise. Don't panic though! Try to split the word into smaller chunks to help you understand its meaning.

Lots of words that come from Latin can be split into prefixes, suffixes and roots. Dividing Latin words up can help you understand their meaning.

Prefix:
trans– means → across

Root:
–port means → carry

So 'transport' means 'carry across'.

Here's a list of prefixes and roots from Latin. Use them to make as many words as you can.

prefixes		roots	
ab–, a–	away from	–dict	speak
circum–	around	–fect	make
con–, co–	together, with	–flect	bend
contra–, contro–	against	–ject	throw
de–	from, down	–mit	send
ex–, e–	from, out	–scribe	write
in–	in, into	–sect	cut
inter–	among, between	–spire	breathe
post–	after, behind	–tain	have, hold
re–	again, back	–tract	drag
sub–	from below, under	–vene	come
super–	above, over	–vert	turn

infect, subject
abject, contain, contract, convert, defect, describe, detain, expire, extract, inflect, inject, inspire, subvert.

Using the tables above, what do you think 'contradict' means?

✎ I think it means to speak against something or someone.

Using the tables above, what do you think 'retain' means?

✎ I think it means to hold back.

Think of the words 'spectacles' and 'spectator'. What do you think 'spect–' means?

✎ I think it means 'look' because a spectator watches.

    © CGP — not to be photocopie

Extension Idea

Get pupils to see how many other words beginning with 'spect' they can think of. Answers might include 'spectacular' or 'spectrum'. Encourage the use of a dictionary for this.

Words From Latin — Aims:

- to demonstrate to pupils how many different Latin roots and prefixes are used in English
- to encourage pupils to consider how meaning is constructed from these roots and prefixes
- to give pupils the opportunity to create words of their own from Latin roots and prefixes.

The words in the table below can be made from a Latin prefix and root. Look at the meaning column, then use the list of Latin prefixes and roots from p12 to help you find the English word.

Meaning	Prefix + Root	English Word
send back	prefix meaning 'back' ↘ re + root meaning 'send' ↙ mit	remit
throw out	e + ject	eject
hold together	con + tain	contain
drag back	re + tract	retract
turn back	re + vert	revert

Look at this dictionary definition of a made-up word.

> short for 'verb'
>
> This is the definition
>
> **circumtract** (*v.*)   to drag around
>
> *Etymology: from Latin 'circum' (around) + 'tract' (drag)*
>
> 'Etymology' shows where the word comes from
>
> *My little sister has a cart which she **circumtracts** everywhere she goes.*
>
> A sentence using the word

Use a Latin prefix and root to make up your own word. Then write your own dictionary entry.

New words are called 'neologisms'. 'Neo' is Greek for 'new'; 'logos' is Greek for 'word'.

> ✏ supervert .... (v)   to turn over
>
> *Etymology:* from Latin 'super' (over) and 'vert' (turn).
> When I superverted my plant pot I found a slug.

How does understanding the meaning of Latin words help you to understand English?

> ✏ If you know the meaning of the different Latin prefixes and roots, it can help you to work out the meaning of words.

Extra Background

Some words from Latin may no longer have their literal meaning. For example, 'conspire' literally means 'breathe together', but we now take it to mean 'join together in a secret act'.

Extension Idea

Ask students to create a list of words whose meanings have changed from the literal meaning. They may need the help of a dictionary.

Suggested Scaffolding

Encourage pupils to think of the English meanings first (using the right-hand columns on page 12), and then fit the translated Latin root and prefix together.

Pupil Guidance

Some children may also recognise that knowing roots and prefixes can help them with spelling.

Saxon Versus Latin

Extra Background

Synonyms are words which have similar meanings, but even synonyms can have different shades of meaning. E.g. synonyms for 'thin' might have positive connotations ('slim') or negative connotations ('gaunt').

Suggested Scaffolding

If pupils get stuck, give them clues by providing them with the opposites. For example, 'the opposite of 'deep' is...'.

Pupil Guidance

Students may wish to use each word in a sentence to see how the meanings vary.

14

Saxon Versus Latin

There are lots of words from Latin which mean pretty much the same thing as words from Saxon. This means that writers have plenty of synonyms to choose from.

Synonyms are different words that have similar meanings.

Use a dictionary or a thesaurus to complete these pairs of synonyms.

From Saxon	From Latin
luck	f o r t u n e
freedom	l i b e r t y
w i s d o m	intelligence
see-through	t r a n s p a r e n t
climb up	a s c e n d
s h a l l o w	superficial

Do these pairs of words mean exactly the same thing? Have a think about how you might use them differently.

Often in English, there are <u>nouns</u> which come from Saxon roots, but the <u>adjective</u> comes from Latin. Fill in this table, using the hints to help you.

Noun from Saxon	Adjective from Latin	Hint
cat	f e l i n e	Latin for cat is 'feles'.
dog	c a n i n e	Latin for dog is 'canis'.
night	n o c t u r n a l	Latin for night is 'nox'.
mother	m a t e r n a l	Latin for mother is 'mater'.
brother	f r a t e r n a l	Latin for brother is 'frater'.
year	a n n u a l	Latin for year is 'annus'.

Section 2 — Ancient Meanings

© CGP — not to be photocopie

Extension Idea

Some of these examples have corresponding adjectives from the Saxon word, e.g. 'nightly', 'brotherly', 'yearly'. Ask pupils to think about where they might use the word 'yearly' and where they might use the word 'annual'. Then discuss whether they have exactly the same meaning.

Saxon Versus Latin — Aims:

- to understand that there are often both Latin and Saxon words for the same thing in English
- to show pupils how using Latin or Saxon words can create different effects in writing.

15

Have another look at the words on the opposite page. Can you come to any conclusions about how words with Saxon roots are <u>different</u> from words with Latin roots?

Words from Saxon tend to be short, common and have fewer syllables. They are used to talk about ordinary, familiar things.

Words from Latin tend to be longer, have more syllables and can be fancy. They are more unusual words.

Use these words to help you:

> "fancy"   "familiar"
> "fewer syllables"
>   "more syllables"
> "unusual"   "common"

Read these descriptions of characters taken from two novels. Look up any words you don't know in the dictionary.

Describing 'Joe' from 'Bleak House' by Charles Dickens:

"**Dirty**, **ugly**, disagreeable to all the senses, in body a common creature of the common streets, only in soul a heathen. Homely **filth begrimes** him, homely parasites devour him, homely **sores** are in him, homely **rags** are on him..."

Describing 'Emma Woodhouse' from 'Emma' by Jane Austen:

"Emma Woodhouse, handsome, clever, and rich, with a **comfortable** home and happy **disposition**, seemed to unite some of the best blessings of **existence**; and had lived nearly twenty-one years in the world with very little to **distress** or **vex** her."

Look at the words in bold. In one text they are from Saxon, in the other they are from Latin. Can you tell which is which? Why might each writer have decided to use these sorts of words?

I think that the description of Joe has Saxon words in it. because the words are short and basic like 'sores', 'ugly' and 'dirty'. The words in 'Emma' are longer, so are probably from Latin. This makes me think that Emma is a more well-spoken character than Joe.

Explain how words from Saxon and Latin give you <u>choices</u> in your writing.

You often have the choice between a word from Saxon or from Latin. Each will give a different feel to your writing.

Section 2 — Ancient Meanings

Pupil Guidance

Many people think that it's impressive to use Latin words whenever possible because it makes their writing sound 'posh' and 'grown-up'. This isn't always the case. Sometimes overusing Latin words can sound a bit pompous, e.g. saying 'unfavourable climatic conditions' instead of 'bad weather.'

Extension Idea

Ask students to rewrite the passage from 'Bleak House' replacing the highlighted words with longer, more unusual words. Then see if they can rewrite the 'Emma' passage, but this time replacing the Latin words with plainer, simpler words.

Suggested Scaffolding

Encourage pupils to look at the length of the bolded words, reminding them that words from Latin tend to be longer.

Pupil Guidance

Pupils should be guided to think about when it might be better to use Latin words and when it might be better to use Saxon ones.

Words From Ancient Greek

Extra Background

Most of the Ancient Greek words we use today actually came into the language through Latin. The Romans valued Ancient Greek over Latin as the language for anything scientific, using Greek terms and ideas in mathematics and science.

Pupil Guidance

Encourage students to write down new words they didn't know before.

Extension Idea

Ask students to create a mind map with a selection of Ancient Greek suffixes from the ones here, along with: '-pod' (foot), '-morph' (form), '-itis' (inflammation or infection) and '-chrome' (colour). They could then write down all the words they know ending with the suffixes before using a dictionary to expand their mind maps.

Words From Ancient Greek

If you can recognise a few prefixes, suffixes and roots from Greek, then you can work out the meanings of lots of unfamiliar words.

Look at these prefixes from Ancient Greek on the scroll. Find two words from the dictionary starting with two different Ancient Greek prefixes, then write down their definitions.

auto– self	neo– new
bio– life	phot– light
duo– two	tech– skill, art
geo– earth	tele– distant
kilo– thousand	therm– heat
micro– small	
mono– single	

My first word is ✏ kilogram

It means one thousand grams.

My second word is biography

It means a piece of writing about someone's life.

Here are some suffixes from Greek. How many words can you think of that end with these suffixes?

–graph write	–scope look at	–onym word, name	–phobia fear of
–mania madness for	–ology study	–meter measuring device	–sophy wisdom

✏ telegraph, autograph, telescope, microscope, synonym, antonym, arachnophobia, pyromania, biology, psychology, technology, thermometer, speedometer, philosophy

---

These groups of words have the same Greek part. Can you figure out what the highlighted part means?

tripod   triangle   tricycle   ✏ Tri means three.

octopus   octagon   octave   Oct means eight.

Section 2 — Ancient Meanings   © CGP — not to be photocopie

Suggested Scaffolding

Ask pupils to think of the number of sides on a triangle, number of wheels on a tricycle, number of legs on an octopus and number of sides on an octagon.

Words From Ancient Greek — Aims:

- to enable pupils to understand that some words have come from Ancient Greek
- to enable pupils to see how words are created from Ancient Greek prefixes and suffixes
- to allow students to derive the meaning of a word by looking at its prefixes and suffixes.

Have a go at decoding these English words using what you know from page 16.

English word	Prefix + suffix	Original meaning
thermometer	therm means 'heat' / meter means 'measuring device' / therm + meter	Heat measuring device
telescope	tele + scope	To see something from afar.
autograph	auto + graph	To write something oneself.
geology	geo + ology	To study the earth.

Can you match up the Greek prefixes and suffixes to the correct meanings?

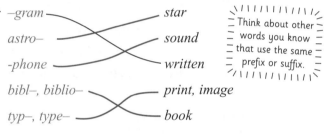

–gram — star
astro– — sound
-phone — written
bibl–, biblio– — print, image
typ–, type– — book

Think about other words you know that use the same prefix or suffix.

Have a go at making up your own Greek word.

My Greek word is ✏ astrogram

It means a message sent from a star.

Now use your word in a sentence.

Make up some more Greek words and get a friend to guess what they mean.

✏ It's expensive to send an astrogram to Earth.

What have you learnt about Greek words from these pages?

✏ I've learnt that we have lots of Greek words in our language.

Extra Background

On occasion, the meanings of the original Ancient Greek words have changed. For example, the literal meaning of the Greek word 'semantic' is 'significant', but today it has the more common meaning of 'relating to the study of language'.

Suggested Scaffolding

Write down a selection of Greek prefixes and suffixes on flashcards to enable students to arrange them as they wish.

Extension Idea

Pupils could use some of their created words in a story. 'Astrogram' for example, would lend itself to a science fiction story. They could combine this with their imaginary animal from the next page as well, to add more interest to their writing.

Pupil Guidance

Pupils may make the leap that lots of the Greek words we use today are scientific or mathematical. This is a perfect introduction to the next page.

More Words From Ancient Greek

18

More Words From Ancient Greek

The Romans thought the Ancient Greeks were amazing so they borrowed lots of their words. When the Romans invaded Britain, they brought some of these words with them.

Look at the words below. They are all English words borrowed from Ancient Greek. What kinds of words are they? What does this tell us about what the Ancient Greeks were like?

> thermometer   poem   music   dynamic   rhyme   democracy
> astronomy   mathematics   philosophy   logical   mythical   theatre
> museum   architect   energy   atmosphere   microscopic   psychology

I think these words tell us that the Ancient Greeks ...... were interested in literature ('poem', 'rhyme', 'theatre'), and in science ('thermometer', 'astronomy', 'energy'). They seem quite intelligent and civilised.

Using what you have learnt about Greek words, look at the words in the box below and circle any that you think have come from Greek.

> (technology)   intersect   deflect   inscribe
> retract   (telephone)
> (photograph)   (kilometre)   (biology)   (synonym)

Think about the meaning of the word 'photograph'. Do you think the Ancient Greeks ever combined the words 'photo' and 'graph' in the same way as today? Explain your answer.

I don't think so because they didn't have cameras or photographs in Ancient Greece.

Can you think of any more words from Greek that have been given to modern inventions?

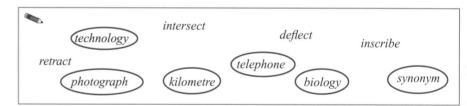

More Words From Ancient Greek — Aims:

- to encourage pupils to consider how Ancient Greek culture and learning impacted the words brought into English via Latin
- to develop pupils' understanding of how and why a common language for science is useful
- to allow pupils to be creative with Greek and Latin roots.

Greek and Latin words are used together to name species of animals and plants. Often the names describe the animal or plant too!

Here's a Globicephala macrorhynchus.

(short-finned pilot whale)

This is from <u>Greek</u>

glob = globe, ball
cephal = head

This is from <u>Latin</u>

macro = large
rhynch = beak, snout

So the name of this whale means 'ball head large snout'.

Scientists around the world use the Latin and Greek names to identify animals and plants. Why do you think this might be useful?

It might be useful because .... it doesn't matter what language they speak, they will still know what the other scientists are talking about. ....

Here are some Greek and Latin words. Can you use them to make up your own species of animal? Draw a picture of your animal in the box below.

Greek	Latin
arctos — bear	glabra — smooth
bradus — slow	hirsutus — hairy
gyrinos — tadpole	maculatus — spotted
lepis — scaly	parvus — small
mauro — black	rufus — red
pod — foot, leg	septem — seven
poly — many	striatus — striped
rhyti — wrinkled	tenuis — thin
saura — lizard	versicolor — multicoloured

My species of animal is called .... Maurobradussaura parvushirsutus ....

It means "black slow lizard small hairy".

....
....

 Read your made-up name to a classmate. Can they describe what your animal looks like?

How have the Ancient Greeks influenced the English language?

They have given us lots of science, art and drama words.

Section 2 — Ancient Meanings

Extra Background

When naming species of animals and plants, the first term is the name of the genus, and the second term denotes the species within the genus. Scientists sometimes make puns out of these. For example, for a beetle whose genus is 'Agra', the biologist Terry Erwin added the species names 'vation' and 'cadabra'.

Suggested Scaffolding

Pupils may prefer to combine some Greek and Latin words at random, and then look at the English words to see what type of creature they have ended up with. It is fine to add or remove a letter, to make the word easier to say out loud.

Extension Idea

Pupils who enjoy this task may like to look at the scientific names of some common animals or plants and consider where they came from and why they were named as they were.

Roaming Register

20 *Section 3 — Wizardly Wordcraft*

Roaming Register

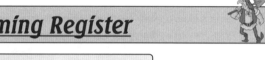

The words you use can make your writing formal or informal — this is called <u>register</u>. The register you use depends on who you're talking to, and what situation you're in.

Can you think of an informal version for each of these words?

Use a thesaurus if you get stuck.

sufficient ⟹ enough

commence ⟹ start

acquire ⟹ get or buy

assist ⟹ help

What about a formal version for these words?

try ⟹ attempt

ask ⟹ request

buy ⟹ purchase

need ⟹ require

Do you think more formal words tend to come from Saxon or Latin roots?

Spoken language has a register too. Think about the different registers you use and fill in these speech bubbles.

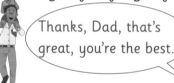

Talking to my family I might say:

Thanks, Dad, that's great, you're the best.

Talking to the Queen I might say:

Thank you, Ma'am, that is kind of Your Majesty.

Write a short letter to complain about a bad meal at a restaurant. Write the first one using <u>informal</u> language and the second one using <u>formal</u> language.

Which one do you think would be more effective?

To Steve,
That meal I had last night was totally gross. I won't come back again. I didn't like the food 'cos it was too spicy and the service was awful. I'd like my money back, OK?

Dear Sir,
I ate at your restaurant last night, and was extremely disappointed in the quality of the food. I would appreciate it if you could refund the money I paid for the dinner.

Section 3 — Wizardly Wordcraft

© CGP — not to be photocopie

Extra Background

Register is something that most people develop without realising.

Suggested Scaffolding

If pupils struggle to understand the idea of register, try a hot-seat exercise where they try to speak to different types of people appropriately (e.g. the Prime Minister, a policeman, a judge, a sibling, a younger child). Ask them if they changed the way they spoke.

Pupil Guidance

More formal words tend to come from Latin roots, whereas informal words tend to originate from Saxon words.

Extension Idea

Register may also extend to different types of language within peer groups. Ask a class to think about whether they speak in a particular way in the classroom. Are there ways in which they speak to each other that they don't use outside the class (or year group)?

Pupil Guidance

Determining whether a letter is more suitable would depend on the occasion. In this case, the more formal letter is likely to be more effective because it shows more respect and so is more likely to be taken seriously.

Roaming Register — Aims:

- to enable pupils to understand the concept of written and spoken register
- to begin to understand what makes a register formal or informal
- to classify texts according to register, and to begin to distinguish registers we use daily.

Look at these three texts below. Who do you think they've been written for?

Text A

Numerous species of reptile inhabit the British Isles. These include several varieties of snake and lizard, alongside the slow-worm which is a legless lizard. All native reptiles are vulnerable, but the slow-worm's limited range and critically endangered habitat make it a more likely candidate for extinction than others.

Text B

Overall Comments: *James has worked hard at his English this year and has achieved his targets. His creative writing has improved, and he is beginning to use a dictionary and a thesaurus to widen his vocabulary. He still needs to work hard at his spelling, as he can sometimes make some very silly mistakes.*

Text C

Dear Roz,

Please come to my party on Saturday 15th at 3pm. Bring your cossie as we're going swimming. We're gonna have a pizza and ice cream after and u can stay over at mine if u want. Mum says she's OK with that so long as we don't keep her up all night. See u soon. Love Ceara xx

Text A has been written for *a science book or information sheet* because *it uses big scientific words and it's formal.*

Text B has been written for *a school report for a parent* because *it uses technical language and is talking about learning.*

Text C has been written for *an informal party invitation to a friend* because *it uses informal language, text-speak and abbreviated words.*

Which of these texts is the most formal? Try to explain your choice.

Text *A* is the most formal text because *it is written in an impersonal style, uses scientific vocabulary, and does not offer any sort of opinion — only facts.*

Think about who you've spoken to today. Which registers have you used?

I spoke to my family informally and my teachers formally.

Pupil Guidance

Text A and B are both written in a fairly formal style, but Text B is a more personal piece of writing, offering an opinion, as well as facts, about its subject.

Pupil Guidance

Different genres of non-fiction writing (such as argument, discussion, persuasion, recount and report) differ in their degree of formality. However, it is not just genre that determines the formality — audience is also important.

Pupils should be aware that it is not correct to use abbreviated or slang speech when writing in the classroom (e.g. in tests) unless using it in the context of fictional writing to demonstrate how one character speaks to another.

Awareness of register, and an ability to change register depending on the context of the spoken or written communication, is an essential part of developing language.

Meandering Meanings

Extra Background

There are three types of irony: verbal, situational (both covered here) and dramatic.

Suggested Scaffolding

Explain to children that they need to think of things that aren't great, wonderful or enjoyable in order to make these sentences ironic.

Suggested Scaffolding

Literal-minded pupils may find it hard to understand verbal irony. Start pupils off by getting them to think about situations that they might see as negative, and how a positive exclamation would make them ironic.

Suggested Scaffolding

Other examples of situational irony might help here, e.g. a fire at a fire station, or a police officer being arrested.

Meandering Meanings

You've probably heard someone say 'no, that's not what I meant', and then explain themselves again more clearly. Sometimes, though, people deliberately don't mean what they say. Let's find out why!

Sometimes people say the <u>opposite</u> of what something really means. This is called <u>IRONY</u>.

"The car's broken down. That's just brilliant."

This is ironic because it's not brilliant at all!

Can you complete these sentences so that they are ironic?

Lucky me, I've ✎ lost my purse again.
Oh great, I banged my head.
How wonderful, you've got mud on the carpet.
I love it when my teacher shouts at me.

Now have a go at writing your own ironic sentences about the topics below.

Homework ➡ ✎ I've been given three hours of homework tonight. I cannot wait!

The dentist ➡ I've got to go to the dentist to get a filling — brilliant!

Something can also be ironic in a situation. Here's a poem all about the sea. It contains irony. Try to spot the ironic sentence and underline it.

"Water, water, everywhere,
And all the boards did shrink;
Water, water, everywhere,
Nor any drop to drink."

S T Coleridge
"The Rime of the Ancient Mariner" (1798)

Why do you think your underlined sentence is ironic?

✎ The sentence says they don't have anything to drink, even though there is water everywhere.

Section 3 — Wizardly Wordcraft

© CGP — not to be photocopie

Pupil Guidance

This is about getting pupils to recognise that irony comes from the contrast — there is water everywhere at sea but the people are still thirsty.

Meandering Meanings — Aims:

- to develop an understanding of what irony is and how it's used
- to consider the purpose and effect of exaggeration and understatement.

Sometimes people say <u>more</u> than they mean. This is called exaggeration, or <u>OVERSTATEMENT</u>.

> *I had to wait forever for my dad to arrive.*

> *My gran is a million years old.*

Can you use exaggeration to complete this sentence?

Do you ever exaggerate?

I'm so hungry I could ✎ eat an elephant cold without salt and vinegar.

Why do people exaggerate sometimes?

✎ Writers often exaggerate to make an effect or to get the readers interested in what they are writing.

Sometimes people say a lot <u>less</u> than they actually mean. This is called <u>UNDERSTATEMENT</u>.

This blizzard is a bit chilly. ⬅ A blizzard is usually freezing, rather than just chilly, so this is an understatement.

Can you underline the understatement in this paragraph?

> *Tia's instructor was very angry. "In the last hour you have managed to burn down half of the huts in the village, collapse all but one of the bridges, and set free a highly dangerous fire-breathing dragon." "Yes," Tia replied nervously, <u>"Maybe I got a tiny bit carried away."</u>*

Why do you think the person in this extract has used understatement?

> *We lost the match 50-0 — it could have gone better.*

I think they said this because ✎ it actually went very badly, and they don't really want to admit it.

Describe a time when you have used words and phrases you didn't really mean.

✎ I once said 'I'm so excited I could burst' when I wouldn't actually burst.

Extension Idea

Children could think of exaggeration starters, e.g. 'I'm so tired I could' and 'I'm so excited I could', then challenge each other to complete them.

Suggested Scaffolding

Many children are told not to exaggerate by parents/ carers. Ask them to look at the actual meaning of what is being said — would they <u>really</u> want to eat an elephant?

Pupil Guidance

Pupils should understand that there's a reason why people don't say what they mean, but that this is different from just lying.

Extension Idea

Next time the pupils write a story, ask them to create a character who has a habit of exaggerating. What sort of thing would they say, and what sort of difficulty could this get them into?

Splendid Similes

24

Extra Background

Some similes seem clichéd now, e.g. 'cold as ice', 'my love's like a red, red rose', but were fresh and inventive when they were originally created.

Extension Idea

Children could use the 'word cloud' method to create similes. Write a word in the centre, e.g. 'silly'. Then surround it with all the ideas that go with the word. Change and rearrange these to create similes for different ways of being 'silly'.

Pupil Guidance

Pupils should think about whether younger children would interpret their similes literally.

Pupil Guidance

This passage has similes in every sentence so that pupils can see how they work. Ask pupils whether you would want this many in a short text, or whether you would be better mixing them with metaphor, e.g. 'The cat, an empress in her finery, padded past...'

Splendid Similes

A <u>simile</u> is a way of describing something by comparing it to something else. Similes use the words 'like' or 'as'.

as sweet as a fresh strawberry   sharp like a shark's tooth

Step 1
Think of an adjective to describe each picture.

Step 2
Think of some other things that could be described with this word.

powerful ➡ a storm   a volcano erupting

bright ➡ a parrot   a scarf

soggy ➡ a wet sponge   muddy ground

Step 3
Now use some of your answers from above to write your own similes. You'll need to use the word 'as' or 'like'.

Try to add some extra details if you can.

The rocket is powerful like a volcano erupting.
The rainbow is as bright as a jungle parrot.
Jim was as soggy as a wet sponge.

Do you think a younger child would understand your similes?

Read the passage below. What do these similes suggest to you about the dog?

The dog was like a shadow in the corner of the room. The cat padded past, like an empress in her finery. The dog cowered under a chair, like a beetle under a rock.

The similes make me think that the dog is quiet and frightened, and not very brave about confronting the cat. It would sooner run and hide.

Section 3 — Wizardly Wordcraft   © CGP — not to be photocopie

Splendid Similes — Aims:

- to get pupils to understand how a simile is formed
- to allow pupils to practise creating similes of their own for a variety of purposes
- to enable pupils to create more complex similes.

Similes can be made better by adding extra details to them. Can you improve these similes?

as fit as an athlete ➡ ✎ as fit as an athlete at the Athletics Championships

as agile as a monkey ➡ as agile as a monkey swinging through the trees

unstable like jelly ➡ unstable like a jelly melting in summer sunshine

Sometimes similes go on to tell you exactly which bits of something they are referring to.

A good book is like a good chair — cosy and welcoming at any time of day.

The writer could just say 'a good book is cosy and welcoming...', but they describe the chair instead so we really imagine being comfortable too.

What does this simile make you think about the inspectors?

"The inspectors were like dust — everywhere and unwanted."

Try not to write 'they are everywhere and unwanted'!

✎ It makes me think they are not very nice people, and they might be a bit dishonest or mean because dust isn't clean.

Similes can be made funny by comparing things to their opposites.

Simone was as welcome as a cat at a dog's birthday party!

This is a funny way of saying Simone was unwelcome.

These similes use irony (take a look at p.22).

Can you think of a funny simile for these things?

Something that isn't quiet ➡ It is as quiet as ✎ a New Year's Eve firework display.

Something that isn't useful ➡ This is as useful as an ice-cube armchair in the Sahara desert.

Something that isn't tasty ➡ This is as tasty as a twelve-month-old ham sandwich.

How can similes make your writing better?

✎ Similes can improve my descriptions, add more details and can also be used to make a funny point.

Suggested Scaffolding

This is a trickier concept (descriptions that seem to defeat the point of the simile), but they focus the reader's attention on specific aspects of the thing described, whilst bringing in other associations. To help children, you could change the second clause from this example and ask them how the meaning has been altered e.g. '...like dust, easy to ignore and easier to clean away.'

Suggested Scaffolding

Encourage the pupils to think of improbable or unworkable things (e.g. a chocolate teapot) and then write a simile around the idea they've had.

Extension Idea

Ask the pupils to create a set of similes for different moods (funny similes, scary similes, beautiful similes), and make them into a display.

Pupil Guidance

All pupils should understand how similes work, but the more able can also mention adding details and humorous elements.

Marvellous Metaphors

Extra Background

The word 'metaphor' comes from a Greek verb 'metapherein' which means 'to transfer'. A metaphor directly transfers characteristics of one thing to the subject of the metaphor. It is more direct than a simile.

Pupil Guidance

Pupils should be careful with metaphors. Shakespeare didn't mean that Juliet was a giant, flaming ball of gas — he expected his readers to use a shared understanding of the beauty and warmth of the Sun when translating his metaphor.

Extension Idea

Get pupils to think of some funny ways to create metaphors, e.g. 'My friend's a lion!' 'What, brave and kingly?' 'No, scruffy, full of fleas, and with very bad breath!'

Marvellous Metaphors

A <u>metaphor</u> is a way of describing something by saying it's something else.

Lena's brother is a pig when he eats.

This isn't true, but it tells you what Lena's brother is <u>like</u> when he eats.

The writer William Shakespeare was a master of metaphor. Read this one from his play 'Romeo and Juliet'. Here, Romeo is talking about his love for Juliet.

"It is the east, and Juliet is the sun."

Why do you think he calls Juliet 'the sun'?

 Juliet might be bright and warm like the Sun.

Use the words below to write some metaphors about people.
Try to use three different colours in each sentence.

at school   uncle   gorilla   on the piano
sister   monster   on holiday   teacher   mum
at home   angel   when hungry   nightmare
dragon   friend   livewire
on the pitch

My sister is an angel at school.
My uncle is a gorilla on the pitch. Mum's a monster from a nightmare. My friend is a dragon when hungry. My teacher is a livewire on the piano.

Can you think of another metaphor using your own words?

Can you write a metaphor about this picture?

Mary is a roaring engine in church.

Suggested Scaffolding

We often use animals in metaphors. Ask the pupils to think of characteristics of animals — snakes can be sneaky, koalas can be cuddly, monkeys can be cheeky — and then use them in metaphors.

Marvellous Metaphors — Aims:

- to get pupils to understand how metaphors are used and how they are different from similes
- to assist pupils in learning how metaphors can be understood
- to allow pupils to play with metaphors in order to enrich their descriptive writing.

27

Metaphors can describe more than one feature at a time. Both of the metaphors below suggest that the wind is quiet, but they tell you something else as well.

> The wind was a gentle whisper.

This metaphor also suggests the wind is calm and peaceful...

> The wind was a whimpering cry.

...but this one suggests it is also sad, or even spooky.

Extension Idea

Read the start of 'The Highwayman' by Alfred Noyes. Ask the pupils how these metaphors make them imagine the wind and the moon.

What do these metaphors suggest to you?

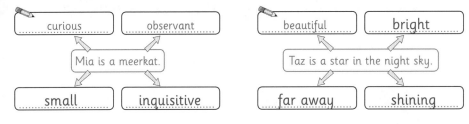

curious	observant

Mia is a meerkat.

small	inquisitive

beautiful	bright

Taz is a star in the night sky.

far away	shining

Pupil Guidance

Different answers should be encouraged, and the point should be made that nobody is wrong.

Are your answers different to other people's? If so, does it mean one of you is wrong?

Think about a character you like from a book or film. Write about what they're like here.

> ✎ I like the character Dorothy in 'The Wonderful Wizard of Oz'. She is a leader, she cheers people up and she is brave.

Suggested Scaffolding

Ask pupils to draw a quick sketch of their character and annotate it with words describing them. By each word, have them put the name of an animal or thing which shares those characteristics. They can use these to create their metaphors.

Can you write some metaphors about them, based on your ideas above? Try to choose metaphors that fit more than one of their characteristics.

Read out your metaphors to a friend. What do they think the character is like?

They are ✎ Dorothy is a light in a sea of darkness.
Dorothy is a breath of fresh air.
Dorothy is a lioness.

I think I will use metaphors to...

✎ make my descriptions better and paint a detailed picture of my characters in my reader's mind.

Section 3 — Wizardly Wordcraft

Pupil Guidance

Pupils don't have to use a character they like — they can use a character they dislike if they prefer, which may be easier to create a metaphor.

Extension Idea

Ask the pupils to create a set of metaphors specifically for evil, dangerous or nasty characters so they can use them when they write.

Incredible Idioms

28

Extra Background

The word 'idiom' comes from the Greek 'idioma' meaning 'a peculiarity' or 'peculiar phraseology'.

Pupil Guidance

Explain to pupils that you don't take idioms literally, and sometimes you just have to know what they mean.

Extension Idea

Ask the pupils to make a list of some idioms they know and illustrate them.

Pupil Guidance

Too many idioms can make your speaking and writing unclear for your audience.

Suggested Scaffolding

If pupils are struggling to think of an answer, give them some idioms from other languages and see if they can understand their meaning. For example, 'it's a carrot' (Korean for 'it's obvious') or 'to hang noodles on his ears' (Russian for 'to tell lies/talk nonsense').

Incredible Idioms

Idioms are phrases that don't mean exactly what they say, but that's OK because lots of people recognise and use them. Idioms only really mean something special to speakers of that language — once they're translated, they can lose their meaning.

Here are some pictures of idioms. Can you work out what they are, and find out what they mean?

"It's raining <u>c a t s</u> and <u>d o g s</u>."

This idiom means   it's raining really heavily.
....

"That'll happen when <u>p i g s f l y</u>!"

This idiom means   something that's very unlikely to happen.

"This is a <u>p i e c e</u> of <u>c a k e</u>."

This idiom means   it's very easy.
....

It's a good idea not to use idioms too often. Why do you think you should be careful when using idioms?

Do you think people learning English as a second language would understand idioms? Explain your answer.

No because if you translate the words literally you still won't get the meaning of the idiom.

Pupil Guidance

Children may answer 'yes', reasoning that you could teach someone what an idiom means. It may be worth drawing their attention to the 'no' reasoning also.

Incredible Idioms — Aims:

- to get pupils to understand what an idiom is
- to get pupils to recognise how idioms are created and when they are used
- to point out to pupils that idioms are best used sparingly, and should not be overused.

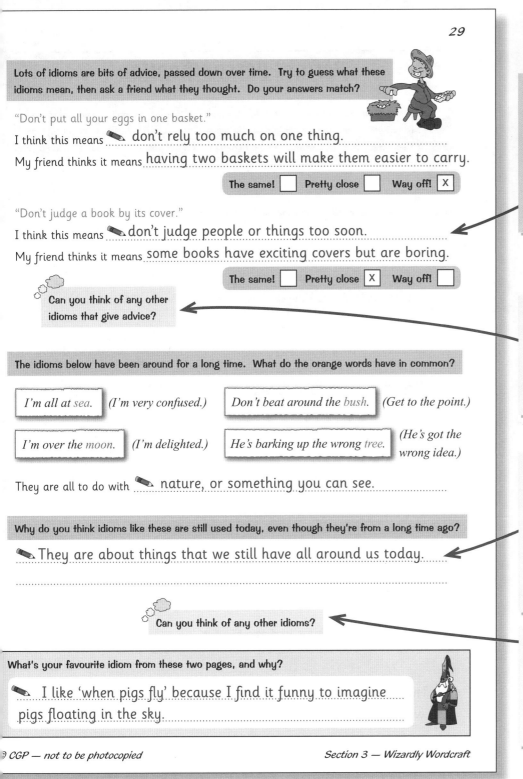

29

Lots of idioms are bits of advice, passed down over time. Try to guess what these idioms mean, then ask a friend what they thought. Do your answers match?

"Don't put all your eggs in one basket."

I think this means don't rely too much on one thing.

My friend thinks it means having two baskets will make them easier to carry.

The same! ☐ Pretty close ☐ Way off! ☒

"Don't judge a book by its cover."

I think this means don't judge people or things too soon.

My friend thinks it means some books have exciting covers but are boring.

The same! ☐ Pretty close ☒ Way off! ☐

Can you think of any other idioms that give advice?

The idioms below have been around for a long time. What do the orange words have in common?

I'm all at sea. (I'm very confused.) *Don't beat around the bush.* (Get to the point.)

I'm over the moon. (I'm delighted.) *He's barking up the wrong tree.* (He's got the wrong idea.)

They are all to do with nature, or something you can see.

Why do you think idioms like these are still used today, even though they're from a long time ago?

They are about things that we still have all around us today.

Can you think of any other idioms?

What's your favourite idiom from these two pages, and why?

I like 'when pigs fly' because I find it funny to imagine pigs floating in the sky.

Section 3 — Wizardly Wordcraft

Suggested Scaffolding

Give pupils the idioms with an accompanying illustration. See if this helps them understand what it means.

Pupil Guidance

Answers might include 'don't bite off more than you can chew' and 'let sleeping dogs lie'.

Pupil Guidance

Pupils may interpret this question differently, and write something like 'they have been handed down over time so they have become very common'.

Pupil Guidance

Other common idioms include 'break a leg', 'I smell a rat' and 'put your foot in it'.

Extension Idea

Let the pupils experiment with creating some idioms of their own. Then allow them to share them with the rest of the class.

Perfect Personification

30

Extra Background

Personification features in many poems. Seasons and weather are commonly personified, as are attributes such as evil, beauty, justice and kindness.

Suggested Scaffolding

If pupils struggle with the specifics of this metaphor, try replacing it with something similar, e.g. 'It was the early afternoon of a stormy day with fierce winds howling at the shutters'.

Extension Idea

Get pupils to look in their reading books to find their own examples of personification. They could make posters of them for the classroom.

Perfect Personification

People are full of feelings. They laugh, they cry, they get excited — and sometimes they get cross. People act in different ways too — rushing, dawdling, snoozing and snoring. When you write about something as if it's a person, it's called **personification**.

Look at the examples of personification below. What words would you use to describe each of the movements? Fill in the gaps, and then complete an example of your own.

slow	heavy		jumpy	...light, gentle

the clouds trudged across the sky   the snowflakes danced in the air

the stream skipped on its way   the ocean gnawed at the beach

happy	playful		fierce	hungry

Here is another example of personification.

It was the early afternoon of a sunshiny day with little winds playing hide-and-seek in it.
K. Mansfield, 'How Pearl Button Was Kidnapped' (1912)

What does this example of personification make you think of?

✎ This makes me think the wind is
playful, or childlike.

> Does it make you think of a certain type of person?

Can you write two more sentences using personification to show how the wind can feel and sound?

> The wind could embrace, caress, press, sting, stab, bellow, murmur, whistle...

Little winds playing hide-and-seek.
✎ The wind murmured in her ear.
The wind bellowed through the hallway when she opened the door.

Section 3 — Wizardly Wordcraft   © CGP — not to be photocopie

---

Pupil Guidance

Using personification like this is also an effective way to show how your character feels about something (in this case, the wind). In the first example here, the wind is gentle. In the second, it is loud and aggressive.

Perfect Personification — Aims:

- to get pupils to recognise that personification gives human characteristics to non-human things
- to assist pupils in using personification in descriptive writing.

Read the extract below. The author is describing the woods.

The woods are whispering between themselves. As the cold wind blows between their branches, they shrug and dance, sending a flurry of needles to the forest floor. I lie here silently, but the knots in the trunks watch me with wooden eyes.

Can you spot the examples of personification used in the text? Write them down here.

✐ The woods are whispering / they shrug and dance / the knots in the trunks watch me with wooden eyes

Suggested Scaffolding

If pupils struggle with this task, ask them to look for the verbs and see if these lead them to examples of personification (e.g. 'whispering', 'shrug', 'dance' and 'watch').

Why do you think writers might use personification?

Personification is brilliant for describing nature.
What sort of things can you see and hear in winter?

✐ frozen skies, pale colours, lots of greys and purples, hear a loud wind, you feel chilled and you have frozen fingers and toes. The wind is cold and sharp.

Pupil Guidance

Answers might include 'to help make their descriptions better'.

Now write a short description of winter using personification.

✐ Sharp-toothed winter roams the icy land.
She is wearing pale snowflakes edged with lacy frost.
Crowned with icicles, she weaves her cruel spells all around.

What sounds like people speaking? What looks like people moving?

Suggested Scaffolding

Pupils may find it easier to draw their idea first and then annotate it with suitable descriptive words.

What have you learnt about personification?

✐ Personification gives human characteristics and feelings to non-human things and objects.

Extension Idea

In this description, winter is a cruel person, perhaps an enchantress or witch. Ask pupils to continue the description with her looks, movement, actions and companions. They could try and write a poem too.

Section 3 — Wizardly Wordcraft

Pupil Guidance

Pupils should understand that personification is another type of figurative language. Some may also mention why it is useful.

Powerful Puzzlers

Extra Background

In the past, people relied on memory, rather than written methods, for storing information. Mnemonics helped them train their memory and remember important information.

Suggested Scaffolding

Ask pupils to look at the picture clues if they're struggling.

Pupil Guidance

Suggest to pupils that it can be helpful to think of something they know well or something that has meaning to them when writing mnemonics — it'll make their mnemonics more memorable.

32

Powerful Puzzlers

"Mnemonics? What are they?" I hear you announce,
"It's a funny old word that I cannot pronounce."
But don't panic yet, they're not really that tough,
And they help you remember some interesting stuff.

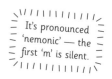
It's pronounced 'nemonic' — the first 'm' is silent.

Mnemonics are clever prompts that help you remember useful information.

Richard Of York Gave Battle In Vain ⇐ This is a mnemonic for the order of colours in the rainbow.

red   orange   yellow   green   blue   indigo   violet

Can you work out what these mnemonics can help you to remember?

Never Eat Soggy Waffles

✎ The order of the points of the compass.

My Very Educated Mother Just Served Us Nachos

The order of the planets from the Sun.

Jack Frost Made A Mess Juggling Juice And Soaked Our Neighbour's Dog
The order of the months.

Can you make up some mnemonics of your own for these things?
You can use the words in any order for these mnemonics.

The five oceans ➡ Pacific   Atlantic   Indian   Southern   Arctic

✎ People And Insects Seem Angry.
Sharks Are Incredible At Painting.

The seven continents ➡ North America   South America   Africa
                                      Asia   Antarctica   Europe   Oceania

✎ Never Eat An Apple On A Slide.
Never Ask An Ostrich About Scrambled Eggs.

Powerful Puzzlers   © CGP — not to be photocopie

Extension Idea

Get students to make their mnemonics into rhymes.   Mnemonics are a chance to have fun and play around with words in a non-serious way.